NORTHWESTERN JOURNAL OF TECHNOLOGY AND INTELLECTUAL PROPERTY

Top Tens in 2011:
Patent and Trademark Cases

Stephen McJohn

January 2012   VOL. 10, NO. 4

© 2012 by Northwestern University School of Law
Northwestern Journal of Technology and Intellectual Property

Top Tens in 2011:
Patent and Trademark Cases

By Stephen McJohn[*]

I. PATENT

The leading development in patent law was the enactment of the Leahy-Smith America Invents Act of 2011.[1] The Act made a number of significant changes in U.S. patent law, such as moving U.S. law closer to most international jurisdictions by shifting to a first-to-file rule for determining priority between competing inventors, instead of first-to-invent;[2] broadening prior user rights; nullifying the best mode requirement; adopting a supplemental examination procedure, to cure defects in an applicants' submissions of prior art; adding a post-grant opposition procedure; and barring patents encompassing centaurs or tax strategies. As to patent reform, meatier issues were addressed by a number of judicial decisions, on such issues as the scope of patent subject matter, challenges to the validity of patents, and the breadth of patent protection.

---

[*] Professor of Law, Suffolk University School of Law. This listing and analysis are decidedly subjective, and all the usual disclaimers apply. Thanks to Heidi Harvey and Joseph Koipally. Comments welcome: smcjohn@suffolk.edu.

[1] Leahy-Smith America Invents Act, Pub. L. No 112-29, 125 Stat. 284–341 (2011) (codified at 35 U.S.C. §§ 2–376). For a clear guide to a complex statute, see Mark A. Lemley, *Things You Should Care About in the New Patent Statute* (Stanford Pub. Law Working Paper No. 1929044, 2011), *available at* http://papers.ssrn.com/sol3/papers.cfm?abstract_id=1929044.

[2] The first-to-invent rules will continue to apply to existing patents and to applications filed until March 17, 2013. The new system might have given a different result in litigation over patent rights to Crestor, a widely sold pharmaceutical. *See* Teva Pharm. Indus. Ltd. v. Astrazeneca Pharm. Indus. LP, 661 F.3d 1378 (Fed. Cir. 2011) (Teva's patent invalidated by Astrazeneca's prior invention date).

313

1. *Association for Molecular Pathology v. U.S. Patent & Trademark Office*, 653 F.3d 1329 (Fed. Cir. 2011) (*Myriad*)

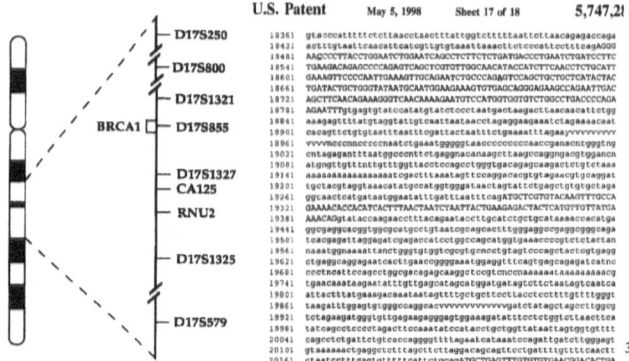

In a case testing the limits of patentable subject matter, the question was whether human genes are patentable. Human genes are not patentable in the form in which they appear in the body, the Federal Circuit stated, because that is a non-patentable "product of nature." But the court held a patent may issue for genes that have been identified and isolated:

> Native DNA exists in the body as one of forty-six large, contiguous DNA molecules. Each DNA molecule is itself an integral part of a larger structural complex, a chromosome.... Isolated DNA, in contrast, is a free-standing portion of a native DNA molecule, frequently a single gene. Isolated DNA has been cleaved... or synthesized to consist of just a fraction of a naturally occurring DNA molecule.[4]

Accordingly, the court upheld Myriad Genetics' patents on isolated *BRCA1* DNA and isolated *BRCA2* DNA, two mutations of human DNA linked to higher probability of breast and ovarian cancer.

The decision also considered process claims related to the genes. The court held that claims on methods of "'comparing' or 'analyzing' two gene sequences" were outside patentable subject matter, because they claimed only "abstract mental processes."[5] The court, however, upheld a claim on "a method for screening potential cancer therapeutics."[6] That claim was patentable, because it had the concrete steps of "growing" host cells, determining their growth rate by manipulating the cells.

The method claim analysis has importance well beyond the issues of the patentability of genes. Whether genes are patentable is important for practical reasons

---

[3] 17Q-Linked Breast & Ovarian Cancer Susceptibility Gene, U.S. Patent 5,747,282 (filed June 7, 1995). To Dennis Crouch's PATENTLY-O, http://www.patentlyo.com, I owe the practice of illustrating patent law cases with relevant patent drawings.
[4] *Myriad*, 653 F.3d at 1351.
[5] *Id.* at 1355.
[6] *Id.* at 1357–58.

(there are thousands of patents on genes) and for theoretical reasons (it triggers questions from philosophy to economics). The process claims may be of more practical importance, because the patentability of processes arises in biotech, but also in many other areas, such as business methods, and software—and software can be in every field. Some abstract software patents are likely to be called into question, if they appear to claim only "abstract mental processes." Where the software has a specific concrete application, it may fall into the second category, making it patentable.

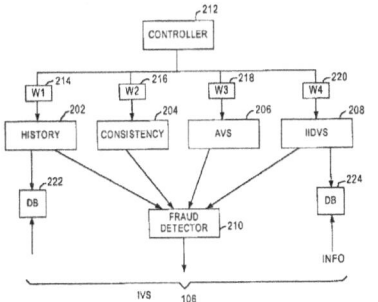

Not long after *Myriad*, the Federal Circuit indeed held a software patent invalid, as claiming an invention that was merely a set of mental steps.[8] Likewise, medical diagnostic procedures and other biotech inventions may be either abstract or concrete. The importance of *Myriad*, however, will become clearer if and when the Supreme Court disposes of *Prometheus*,[9] now pending before the Supreme Court, which deals with the patentability of a diagnostic procedure.

The 2011 Leahy-Smith America Invents Act provided a specific limitation on patentable subject matter in life sciences: "Notwithstanding any other provision of law, no patent may issue on a claim directed to or encompassing a human organism."[10] The provision would bar patents on genetically altered humans and cloned humans, and very likely chimeras combining humans and other species (not that any actual inventions were in sight as of the date of the statute). Read broadly, the provision could apply to human stem cell methods or products, or even other inventions involving human cells. Because "directed to" and "encompassing" are not defined terms, it could in theory be read very broadly indeed. Any method of medical treatment, fitness program, or weight loss method is directed to a human organism, in a sense, especially if the effects on the subject range throughout the body. "Encompassing a human organism," literally, could encompass a game of Ring a Ring o' Roses. The United States Patent and Trademark Office (USPTO), however, soon stated its view that the provision simply codified

---

[7] U.S. Patent No. 6,029,154 (filed July 28, 1997).
[8] *See* CyberSource Corp. v. Retail Decisions Inc., 654 F.3d 1366 (Fed. Cir. 2011).
[9] Mayo Collaborative Servs. v. Prometheus Labs., 628 F.3d 1347 (Fed. Cir. 2010), *cert. granted*, 131 S. Ct. 3027 (U.S. June 20, 2011) (No. 10–1150).
[10] Leahy-Smith America Invents Act, Pub. L. No 112-29, § 33, 125 Stat. 284, 340 (2011). This provision, counterparts of which had been including in previous budget legislation, was not codified into the Patent Act.

existing USPTO policy.[11] Although that policy has likewise not been set out in detail, the USPTO has issued many patents on human genes (hence *Myriad*), human cells, and other human biotech inventions; so, such patents will continue to issue, unless the courts read the patent statute otherwise.

The 2011 patent legislation also effectively barred statutes on "any strategy for reducing, avoiding, or deferring tax liability."[12] The section provides that it does not bar patents on methods or computerized systems for preparing tax returns or for financial management (not that such business methods are necessarily patentable, the section further provides).

2. *Microsoft Corp. v. i4i Limited Partnership*, 131 S. Ct. 2238 (2011)

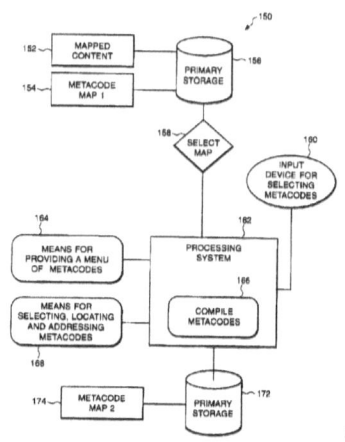

13

A patent should not issue if the claimed invention is not new. But showing that something had been done before is not always easy. With software patents especially, it may be difficult to find code (which is often not widely available) that prefigures a subsequent patent. Something that complicates the issue is that once the patent is issued, it is presumed valid, and can only be invalidated with "clear and convincing" evidence. That gives a lot of leverage to patent holders. When an inventor applies for a patent, the examiner must decide if the invention has already been sold or commercially used in the United States or published anywhere in the world. The examiner, however, has limited resources to look for all those possible references.

Microsoft argued that the standard should be adjusted. Where a party presented evidence that had not been considered by the patent examiner, a court could use the general "preponderance" standard: if it was more likely than not that the patent was wrongly issued, it would be held invalid. In patent litigation, parties often uncover

---

[11] Memorandum from Robert Bahr, Senior Patent Counsel, U.S. Patent & Trademark Office, to Patent Examining Corps (Sept. 20, 2011) (stating that "section 33(a) of the Leahy-Smith America Invents Act codifies existing USPTO policy that human organisms are not patent-eligible subject matter").
[12] Leahy-Smith America Invents Act § 14. This provision was also not codified into the Patent Act.
[13] U.S. Patent No. 5,787,449 (filed June 2, 1994).

relevant references not considered during the application process. Compared to a single examiner, a patent defendant has much greater incentives, as millions of dollars may be at stake, and resources to research whether the invention was truly new. The Supreme Court, however, declined to depart from the existing standard, leaving it to Congress to change the patent statute if it so chose. Notably, Congress did not make this reform in the 2011 patent legislation.

3. *Global-Tech. Appliances, Inc. v. SEB S.A.*, 131 S. Ct. 2060 (2011)

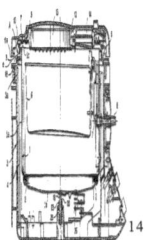

The Supreme Court also addressed the issue of when a party may be liable for infringement by someone else. Pentalpha copied an SEB deep fryer, whose cool-touch technology was a commercial success. Pentalpha then had an attorney analyze whether Pentalpha's fryer infringed any patents—but without informing the attorney that the fryer was made by copying SEB's fryer. Pentalpha exported the fryer to various retailers. The retailers infringed by selling the fryer. The question was whether Pentalpha was secondarily liable for causing them to sell the infringing fryer.

When should one be liable for infringement by another? The patent statute requires knowledge of the infringement for secondary liability.[15] In *Global-Tech Appliances*, the Supreme Court held that "willful blindness" to infringement is sufficient to meet the knowledge requirement. Pentalpha did not know that its fryer infringed the SEB fryer. Indeed, its attorney had not discovered any patents that that the Pentalpha fryer infringed. But had the attorney been advised that the fryer was copied from SEB, it's much more likely the attorney would have looked at the SEB patent and advised otherwise. After deliberately insulating itself from knowledge of patent infringement, Pentalpha could not argue that lack of knowledge protected it from infringement liability.

An ironic footnote: a premise of the Court's analysis is that simply asking an attorney to examine a product and compare it to the data base of existing patents is not a dependable way to see if a product is likely to infringe a patent. In other words, the Court assumes that patents do not provide much notice to potential infringers (whether willfully blind, as Pentalpha was in *Global-Tech Appliances*, or innocent, as in the typical case).

---

[14] U.S. Patent No. 4,995,312 (filed Aug. 28, 1990).
[15] 35 U.S. 271(b) (2006).

4. *Board of Trustees of the Leland Stanford Junior University v. Roche Molecular Systems*, 131 S. Ct. 2188 (2011)

United States Patent [19]	[11] Patent Number:	5,968,730
Merigan et al.	[45] Date of Patent:	Oct. 19, 1999

[54] POLYMERASE CHAIN REACTION ASSAYS FOR MONITORING ANTIVIRAL THERAPY AND MAKING THERAPEUTIC DECISIONS IN THE TREATMENT OF ACQUIRED IMMUNODEFICIENCY SYNDROME

[75] Inventors: Thomas C. Merigan, Portola Valley; David A. Katzenstein, Menlo Park; Mark Holodniy, Mountain View, all of Calif.

[73] Assignee: Leland Stanford Junior University, Palo Alto, Calif.

[21] Appl. No.: 08/470,885

[22] Filed: Jun. 6, 1995

Related U.S. Application Data

The Bayh-Dole Act of 1980 has led to considerable commercial development of university research. The Act sets up a framework, under which universities may elect to patent inventions made through federally funded research, or may allow the researchers to seek patents on the inventions. The narrow issue in *Board of Trustees of the Leland Stanford Junior University v. Roche Molecular Systems* was whether the patent rights vest automatically in the university, or only after the researcher makes the required assignment of patent rights. The Supreme Court held that the general rule in patent law applies: the inventor initially has the right to patent, which passes only after an effective assignment has been made (even if, as in Bayh-Dole, the inventor is required to make that assignment).

The Court did not address a broader issue of patent licensing that arose in the case. Courts differentiate between an agreement assigning patent rights and a promise to assign patent rights. The latter does not actually assign the rights; a second agreement actually assigning the rights must be executed. Some have questioned whether that accurately reflects patent law's historical approach or the intent of the parties. It is rare that the parties would intend anything other than an assignment of the rights effective at the time the initial agreement is made, as opposed to a commitment to sit down again later and sign the rights over. So, drafting licensing agreements retains that trap for the unwary.

---

[16] U.S. Patent No. 5,968,730 (filed June 6, 1995).

5. *Therasense, Inc. v. Becton, Dickinson & Co.*, 649 F.3d 1276 (Fed. Cir. 2011) (en banc)

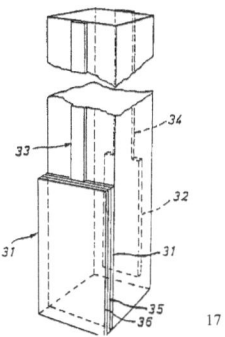

A patent applicant is not required to search to see if her invention is new and nonobvious, and is not required to submit information on the relevant technology to the patent office. But she does have a duty to submit information on whatever relevant technology she is aware of. If the applicant fails to do so, the patent may be held unenforceable. *Therasense* addressed the consequences of failing to disclose. A meandering line of cases had set confusing standards on the issue of when a patent would be unenforceable due to failure to disclose. Some cases have held patents unenforceable, even where the non-disclosed information would have had little effect or the failure to disclose reflected little intent to mislead the USPTO. The majority of defendants in patent litigation raised inequitable conduct as a defense.[18]

The en banc court raised the bar: "This court now tightens the standards for finding both intent and materiality in order to redirect a doctrine that has been overused to the detriment of the public."[19] The court set high standards of proof for both the applicant's state of mind and the materiality of the non-disclosed material. As to state of mind, "the accused infringer must prove that the patentee acted with the specific intent to deceive the [US]PTO."[20] The nondisclosure must also generally involve highly relevant information, such that the "[US]PTO would not have allowed a claim had it been aware of the undisclosed prior art."[21] Given those high standards, inequitable conduct is now a much less promising defense. Indeed, in most cases, it would require showing prior art that would invalidate the patent anyway for obviousness or lack of novelty. The 2011 patent statute provided for a supplemental examination procedure, in which a patentee could submit material that had not been submitted during prosecution of the patent and thereby

---

[17] Strip Electrode with Screen Printing, U.S. Patent No. 5,820,551 (filed Oct. 13, 1998).
[18] Ad Hoc Comm. on Rule 56 and Inequitable Conduct, Am. Intellectual Prop. Law Ass'n , *The Doctrine of Inequitable Conduct and the Duty of Candor in Patent Procurement* (cited in *Therasense*, 649 F.3d at 1288, for its finding that eighty percent of patent cases involve allegations of inequitable misconduct).
[19] *Therasense*, 649 F.3d at 1290.
[20] *Id.*
[21] *Id.* at 1291.

not be subject to a finding of inequitable conduct.[22] Given that *Therasense* moots most such cases, the supplemental examination will be less important strategically, but still provides a procedure to clear the record.

6. *Centocor Ortho Biotech, Inc. v. Abbott Laboratories*, 636 F.3d 1341 (Fed. Cir. 2011)

```
<210> SEQ ID NO 19
<211> LENGTH: 20
<212> TYPE: DNA
<213> ORGANISM: Artificial Sequence
<220> FEATURE:
<223> OTHER INFORMATION: PCR oligonucleotides

<400> SEQUENCE: 19

atcggacgtg gacgtgcaga                                        20
```

What is claimed is:
1. An isolated recombinant anti-TNF-α antibody or antigen-binding fragment thereof, said antibody comprising a human constant region, wherein said antibody or antigen binding fragment (i) competitively inhibits binding of A2 (ATCC Accession No. PTA-7045) to human TNF-α, and (ii) binds to a neutralizing epitope of human TNF-α in vivo with an affinity of at least 1×10⁸ liter/mole, measured as an association constant (Ka), as determined by Scatchard analysis.

of A2 (ATCC Accession No. PTA-7045), and (ii) binds to a neutralizing epitope of human TNF-α in vivo with an affinity of at least 1×10⁸ liter/mole, measured as an association constant (Ka), as determined by Scatchard analysis.

8. A composition comprising the antibody or antigen-binding fragment of claim 1, and a pharmaceutically acceptable carrier.

9. The antibody or antigen-binding fragment of claim 1, which has specificity for a neutralizing epitope of human TNF-α.[23]

The written description requirement acts as a safeguard against overbroad claims. It also serves to balance the timing issues of patent prosecution. A patent applicant must provide a written description of the invention, as well as claims that define the invention. The applicant may amend the claims during the process of patent prosecution. That way, if the USPTO denies the application because the claims are too broad or otherwise defective, the applicant may amend the claims in order to receive a patent. Otherwise, deserving inventors might be denied patents simply because they did not draft claims that were deemed acceptable. But the ability to amend claims raises some hazards. An applicant may amend claims in order to cover the processes or products of others that became public after the application was filed. At its extreme, "submarine patenting" involved amending patent applications decades after they were filed, to cover after-developed technology.[24] But less dramatic cases also show the hazards of amending claims. Centocor filed a patent application on a pharmaceutical, a mouse antibody targeted at treating arthritis. Abbott, a competitor, subsequently marketed a pharmaceutical for treating arthritis, based on a similar human antibody. Centocor amended its patent claims in the pending application to cover human antibodies, obtained a patent, and sued for infringement. A jury awarded $1.67 billion in damages.

---

[22] Leahy-Smith America Invents Act, Public L. No 112-29, § 12, 125 Stat. 284, 325 (2011) (codified at 35 U.S.C. § 257 (2011)).

[23] U.S. Patent 7,070,775 (filed July 18, 2002).

[24] "Submarine patenting" refers to the tactic of an applicant deliberately delaying the issuance of a patent, meanwhile amending its claims, in order to cover technology developed after the patent application was filed. The practice is now less likely for two reasons. *See* STEPHEN M. MCJOHN, INTELLECTUAL PROPERTY: EXAMPLES AND EXPLANATIONS (3rd ed. 2009). First, for applications filed after 1995, the patent term starts running from the application date. Second, the Federal Circuit began to apply the doctrine of prosecution estoppels, which would bar enforcement of a patent, where unreasonable delay was shown in prosecution of the application. *See* Symbol Techs., Inc. v. Lemelson Med. 277 F.3d 1361 (Fed. Cir. 2002).

The Federal Circuit overturned the award, reasoning that the claims were invalid, as not supported by the written description. The written description requirement applies to the application as of the date of application. It therefore acts as a limitation on an applicant's ability to amend the claims during the application. Centocor did not meet the written description requirement for a human antibody by identifying the properties of a mouse antibody in the application, even if it did disclose that the method might subsequently be developed to produce a human antibody. Accordingly, the description did not support the subsequent amendment to the claims in the patent application.

Other notable cases in 2011 turned on the written description requirement. Johnson and Johnson patents (like Centocor's, with claims amended long after the filing of the application) were invalidated as failing to describe the claimed angioplasty stents.[25] A patent on method for detecting genetic mutations related to iron absorption disorders was held to merely describe a "research plan" as of the filing date, as opposed to supporting the claimed diagnostic method.[26] By contrast, a patent for an improved form of soda can survived an invalidity challenge, even though it did not address all the technical challenges described in the application.[27]

---

[25] *See* Boston Scientific Corp. v. Johnson & Johnson, 647 F.3d 1353 (Fed. Cir. 2011).

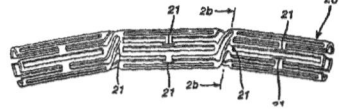

U.S. Patent No. 7,217,286 (filed Aug. 24, 2006).

[26] *See* Billups-Rothenberg, Inc. v. Associated Reg'l & Univ. Pathologists, 642 F.3d 1031 (Fed. Cir. 2011); *see also* Jason Rantanen, Billups-Rothenberg v. ARUP: *The Dangers of Filing Too Early . . . or Too Late*, PATENTLY-O (May 3, 2011), http://www.patentlyo.com/patent/2011/05/billups-rothenberg-v-arup-dont-file-too-earlyor-too-late.html (showing how races to develop a new technology may lead to inventors filing too soon (because they cannot yet sufficiently describe the invention) or too late (because others have gained patent rights or publicly disclosed the invention, making it unpatentable)).

[27] *See* Crown Packaging Tech. Inc. v. Ball Metal Beverage Container Corp., 635 F.3d 1373 (Fed. Cir. 2011).

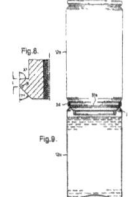

U.S. Patent No. 6,848,875 (filed Dec. 18, 2001).

7. *Eon-Net LP v. Flagstar Bancorp*, 653 F.3d 1314 (Fed. Cir. 2011)

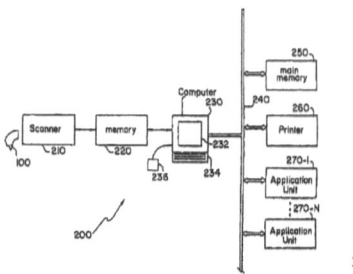

28

¶20 The Federal Circuit affirmed sanctions for baseless patent litigation. Eon-Net filed a baseless case, failed to make a reasonable pre-suit investigation, destroyed evidence before filing the suit, and engaged in obstructive conduct during the case. The court also took into account that the party was simply seeking licensing revenue and was not an active participant in the market—because such a party would be affected by the uncertainties of litigation. The court also noted that Eon-Net had filed numerous suits and settled for small fractions of the likely cost of litigation, indicating that it might have little confidence in the validity of the claims. *Eon-Net* makes it a little more risky to try to enforce patents beyond their scope.

¶21 On the topic of professional responsibility: a question for 2012 will be where to litigate legal malpractice claims involving patents. The Federal Circuit signaled that it may reconsider whether federal courts can hear such cases. The Texas Supreme Court, meanwhile, held that state courts cannot, potentially leaving such cases vagabond.[29]

---

[28] U.S. Patent No. 6,683,697 (filed Dec. 9, 1999).
[29] *Compare* Byrne v. Wood, Herron & Evans LLP, No. 2011-1012, 2011 WL 5600824 (Fed. Cir. Nov. 18, 2011) (stating in dicta that "we believe this court should re-evaluate the question of whether jurisdiction exists to entertain a state law malpractice claim involving the validity of a *hypothetical* patent, " in case where inventor argued that law firm "was negligent in failing to secure broader patent protection for his invention") *with* Minton v. Gunn, No. 10-0141, 2011 WL 6276121 (Tex. Dec. 16, 2011) (holding that "federal courts possess exclusive subject-matter jurisdiction over state-based legal malpractice claims that require the application of federal patent law," in case where plaintiff alleged that "negligent failure to timely plead and brief the experimental use exception to the on-sale bar cost him the opportunity of winning his federal patent infringement litigation").

8. *In re Aoyama*, 656 F.3d 1293 (Fed. Cir. 2011); *Typhoon Touch Technologies, Inc. v. Dell, Inc.*, 659 F.3d 1376 (Fed. Cir. 2011); *Star Scientific, Inc. v. R.J. Reynolds Tobacco Co.*, 537 F.3d 1357 (Fed. Cir. 2011)

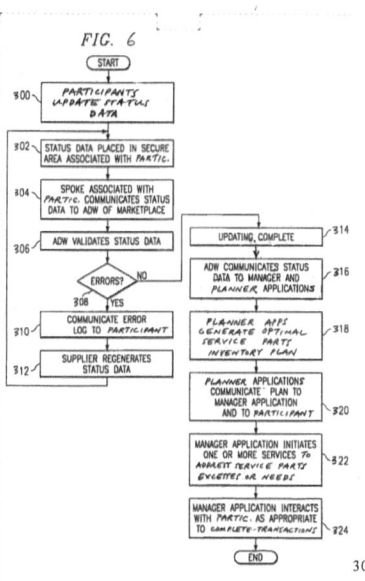

The claims of a patent define the scope of the rights in the invention. If the claims are indefinite, they fail to give others notice of what products or processes would infringe the patent. Software patents have often been criticized as having claims that are too abstract, that could read on software far from the actual invention.[31] *Aoyama* invalidated a software patent for failing to provide sufficient description of the claimed invention. Specifically, a flow chart that described part of the process at a high level did not provide sufficient structure to describe the means included in the patent claim. By contrast, *Typhoon Touch* held a claim for a portable, keyboardless computer provided sufficient structure, where the algorithm for the claimed method was described in prose in the written description. Along those lines, in *Star Scientific,* a patent on a process for curing tobacco was not indefinite, even though it did not provide numerical values for several variables used in the process.[32] Rather, because tobacco curing is "more of an art than a science,"[33] the court reasoned that one skilled in the art would have sufficient information to implement the method.

---

[30] U.S. Patent Application Publication No. 2001/0034673 (filed Feb. 21, 2001).
[31] *See generally*, JAMES BESSEN & MICHAEL J. MEURER, PATENT FAILURE: HOW JUDGES, BUREAUCRATS, AND LAWYERS PUT INNOVATORS AT RISK (2008).
[32] *Star Scientific*, 537 F.3d at 1374.
[33] *Id.* at 1380 (Dyk, Circuit Judge, concurring in part, dissenting in part).

9. *Western Union Co. v. MoneyGram Payment Systems, Inc.*, 626 F.3d 1361 (Fed. Cir. 2011); *Innovention Toys, LLC v. MGA Entertainment, Inc.*, 637 F.3d 1314 (Fed. Cir. 2011)

A claimed invention is not patentable if it was obvious in light of the prior art—existing relevant known technology. Much technology is being adapted for online use. *Western Union* held it obvious to simply adapt funds transfer system using telephones and faxes to an Internet implementation. *Innovention* looked in the opposite direction. In defining the relevant technology to assess the obviousness of a board game, electronic versions of similar games were held to be analogous technology, included within the obviousness analysis.

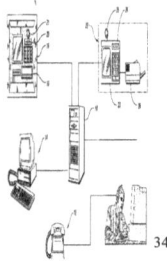

10. *Uniloc USA, Inc. v. Microsoft Corp.*, 632 F.3d 1292 (Fed. Cir. 2011)

The Federal Circuit in *Uniloc* rejected the twenty-five percent "rule of thumb," as a presumptive measure of the percentage of an infringer's profits to be awarded as damage, as "a fundamentally flawed tool."[35] Especially in computer technology, where a product may touch on thousands of patents, rules geared toward the actual damages work better than automatic rules.

II. PATENT PENDING

- *Mayo Collaborative Services v. Prometheus Laboratories, Inc.*, 628 F.3d 1347 (Fed. Cir. 2010), *cert. granted*, 131 S. Ct. 3027 (2011), took the following question on review:

    Whether 35 U.S.C. § 101 is satisfied by a patent claim that covers observed correlations between blood test results and patient health, so that the claim effectively preempts all uses of the naturally occurring correlations, simply because well-known methods used to administer prescription drugs and test blood may involve 'transformations' of body chemistry.

- *Kappos v. Hyatt*, 625 F.3d 1320 (Fed. Cir. 2010), *cert. granted*, 131 S. Ct. 3064 (2011) (whether patent applicant, appealing denial of patent, may introduce new evidence in district court).

---

[34] U.S. Patent No. 6,488,203 (filed Oct. 26, 1999).
[35] *Uniloc*, 632 F.3d at 1315.

- *Caraco Pharmaceutical Laboratories, Ltd. v. Novo Nordisk A/S*, 601 F.3d 1359 (Fed. Cir. 2010), *cert. granted*, 131 S. Ct. 3057 (2011) (whether generic drug manufacturer may file counterclaim seeking correction of patent information).

III. PENDING EN BANC BEFORE FEDERAL CIRCUIT:

- *Akamai Technologies v. Massachusetts Institute of Technology*, 419 F. App'x. 989 (Fed. Cir. 2011).
- *McKesson Technologies v. Epic Systems Corp.*, No. 2010-1291, 2011 WL 2173401 (Fed. Cir. May 26, 2011) (whether actions of multiple parties, taken together, may infringe patent).

IV. TRADEMARK

Trademark cases tested the borders of trademark protection—distinctiveness and functionality, along with the interplay between trademark law and other areas of the law, such as the First Amendment, products liability, and Internet domain name ownership.

1. *Lou v. Otis Elevator Co.*, 933 N.E.2d 140 (Mass. App. Ct. 2010)

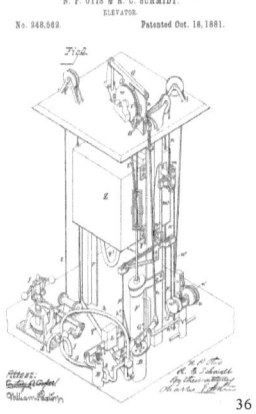
36

Lou v. Otis Elevator is not strictly a trademark law case, nor was it decided in 2011. But it reminds trademark owners and plaintiff's lawyers of a doctrine with considerable practical importance, under which trademark licensors may be liable for defective products sold by licensees. Under the "apparent manufacturer" doctrine, the trademark owner may be liable for injuries caused by goods bearing its licensed mark, provided it participated substantially in the design, manufacture, or distribution of the products. Otis Elevator Company was liable for injuries caused by an escalator made by an overseas joint venture, where Otis Elevator provided its marks and technology under a license. In an era when licensing transactions are increasingly common, trademark owners

---

[36] U.S. Patent No. 248,562 (filed Apr. 8, 1881).

frequently rely on manufacturers who can produce the goods at lower costs, sometimes in other jurisdictions. Trademark owners should know that a licensing transaction is not simply a one-way agreement that brings in revenue. It also brings in legal risks analogous to those that the trademark owner would have if it manufactured the goods itself—legal risks created by products liability, breach of warranty, and consumer protection law. In short, a trademark owner is not able to simply take the benefits of commercializing a symbol on which consumers rely without taking responsibility for how that symbol is used to communicate with consumers.

2. *Eva's Bridal Ltd. v. Halanick Enterprises, Inc.*, 639 F.3d 788 (7th Cir. 2011)

A trademark is a symbol that distinguishes one source of goods and services. A trademark owner may license use of the mark to others, but must maintain some control over the use of the mark. Otherwise, the symbol will not act as a source-identifier. Courts have been extremely forgiving, however, in analyzing whether a trademark holder has abandoned the mark by failing to control its use. *Eva's Bridal* represents a rare decision finding abandonment. The licensor exercised no control at all over how the licensee used the mark. The licensor did not control the marketing of goods or appearance of the retail operation. Accordingly, the trademark owner could not recover unpaid licensing royalties.

3. *Fair Isaac Corp. v. Experian Information Solutions, Inc.*, 650 F.3d 1139 (8th Cir. 2011)

A symbol that merely describes goods or services is not protectable as a trademark, unless such trademark obtains secondary meaning. Because a mark is "merely descriptive," prospective buyers may not regard it as a source-identifying symbol. More importantly, if one competitor held a trademark on a merely descriptive term, that would limit the ability of other competitors to describe their wares to prospective buyers. The store of potential trademark symbols is infinite, so there is little cost in denying trademark protection to merely descriptive symbols. *Fair Isaac* held that "300-850" was merely descriptive of the relevant credit-scoring business, and therefore was not protectable as a mark.

---

[37] Peasant Wedding Procession, Peter Brueghel the Younger (1564-1637).

4. *Georgia–Pacific Consumer Products LP v. Kimberly–Clark Corp.*, 647 F.3d 723 (7th Cir. 2011)

Even a distinctive symbol may not be a trademark, if it is functional. This rule polices the boundary between trademark and patent. Functional matter may be protected only subject to patent's high requirements for protection and limited duration. *Georgia–Pacific* held that a "Quilted Diamond Design" used on toilet paper was functional.[39] In reaching that decision, the court relied on several related patents held by the trademark owner, which discussed the functional advantages of the design: "Thus, reading the language of the patents, we find that the 'central advance' claimed in the utility patents is embossing a quilt-like diamond lattice filled with signature designs that improves (perceived) softness and bulk, and reduces nesting and ridging."[40]

5. *Fleischer Studios, Inc. v. A.V.E.L.A.*, Inc., 636 F.3d 1115 (9th Cir. 2011)

Testing the bounds of the functionality doctrine, the Ninth Circuit adopted the doctrine of "aesthetic functionality."[41] Broadly applied, that would allow others to use a trademark where the trademark itself was something consumers sought. Perhaps anyone could sell Chicago Cubs hats, where consumers regard "Chicago Cubs" as a product feature. The court shortly thereafter withdrew the opinion and resolved the case on narrower grounds,[42] leaving trademark lawyers feeling, as one practitioner put it to me, "like almost getting hit by a bus or something!"

6. *TrafficSchool.com, Inc. v. Edriver Inc.*, 653 F.3d 820 (9th Cir. 2011)

TrafficSchool.com represents an increasing attention among courts to the restrictions on free speech arising from remedies for intellectual property infringement. Courts in copyright cases have become less ready to grant injunctions against infringers, where damages are available to redress harms, because of the speech-inhibiting effect of injunctions. In *TrafficSchool.com*, the trial court had ordered a web site to display a

---

[38] *Georgia–Pacific*, 647 F.3d at 726.
[39] *Id.* at 732.
[40] *Id.* at 729.
[41] *Fleischer Studios*, 636 F.3d at 1124.
[42] Fleischer Studios, Inc. v. A.V.E.L.A., Inc., 654 F.3d 958, 958 (9th Cir. 2011).

disclaimer to all users. The appellate court directed the trial court to properly consider the burden on speech.

7. *Network Automation, Inc. v. Advanced Systems Concepts, Inc.*, 638 F.3d 1137 (9th Cir. 2011)

Trademark law has proven quite resilient, using long-established doctrine to handle the novel fact patterns generated by online communication and technology. *Network Automation* shows that the same basic concerns arise online as in reality. The mark holder had sued a competitor for using its mark for keyword advertising with Google. An influential early case, *Brookfield Communications, Inc. v. West Coast Entertainment Corp.*,[43] had identified three factors as key in the Internet context for determining if there was the requisite likelihood of confusion for trademark infringement: how similar the marks are, how related the goods are, and whether both companies use the Internet as a marketing channel. The trial court focused on those factors in finding infringement. The appellate court, however, held that the court should apply the same factors as in infringement cases generally, in a flexible manner.

8. *Levi Strauss & Co. v. Abercrombie & Fitch Trading Co.*, 633 F.3d 1158 (9th Cir. 2011)

[44]

After almost disappearing in wake of *Moseley v. V Secret Catalogue, Inc.*[45] (in which the Supreme Court considerably narrowed its scope), the dilution cause of action has made a considerable comeback. Congress reacted to *Moseley* by lowering the proof requirement,[46] and courts have broadly applied dilution. *Levi Strauss* continues that trend. In a change from previous dilution law, the court held that a junior mark need not be "identical or nearly identical" to the senior mark to give rise to dilution. The court reasoned that in amending the dilution statue to make proof of dilution easier, Congress also implicitly broadened dilution to reach marks that are not nearly identical to the plaintiff's famous mark. Dilution, a broad protection given to famous marks, becomes a

---

[43] 174 F.3d 1036 (9th Cir. 1999).
[44] *Levi Strauss*, 633 F.3d at 1175–76.
[45] 537 U.S. 418 (2003).
[46] 15 U.S.C. § 1125(c) (2006).

more useful tool. In practical terms, that means that businesses of every type may be well advised to think thrice before using symbols that are at all similar to famous marks—a troubling effect on speech.

9. *Newport News Holdings Corp. v. Virtual City Vision, Inc.*, 650 F.3d 423 (4th Cir. 2011)

Often, a registered domain name is uncomfortably similar to a trademark. The trademark owner has two legal avenues: arbitration under the Uniform Domain Name Dispute Resolution Policy, in which the trademark owner seeks to have the domain handed over; and litigation under the Anticybersquatting Consumer Protection Act, in which the trademark owner seeks the domain and a monetary award. There are many reasons a domain might resemble a trademark (coincidence, comment, parody, prior use, etc.), so both procedures require the complainant to show bad faith. *Newport News* shows that the two are not mutually exclusive.

Newport News, a women's clothing line, pursued an arbitration proceeding, seeking the domain Newportnews.com, which was used for news in the Newport News, Virginia area. The arbitration panel found no bad faith, given the dissimilarity between the two markets (clothing and news). In following years, Newportnews.com, while offering to sell the domain to Newport News, shifted its focus from news to women's clothing. The court found bad faith and awarded damages and attorney's fees. *Newport News* shows that winning the right to retain a domain does not give carte blanche for use of that domain.

www.ingramcontent.com/pod-product-compliance
Lightning Source LLC
Chambersburg PA
CBHW021857170526
45157CB00006B/2486